American Culture

Jeanne Dustman M.A.Ed.

Consultant

Caryn Williams, M.S.Ed.
Madison County Schools
Huntsville, AL

Image Credits: p.7 (right) IS786/Image Source/Alamy; pp.26 (top), 32 Peter Casolino/Alamy; p.16 David Bleeker Photography/Alamy; p.19 (left) Susan Isakson/Alamy; p.23 (top) Jon Feingersh/Blend Images/Alamy; p.17 (top) flab/Alamy; p.23 (right) Bob Daemmrich/Alamy; p.13 (top) Tim Graham/Alamy; p.5 Justin Green/Alamy; p.24 (left) The Bridgeman Art Library; p.21 (left) Bettmann/Corbis; p.18 CSA Images/Vetta/Getty Images; p.26 (bottom) Tim Bieber/Digital Vision/Getty Images; p.29 (top) Indeed/Getty Images; p.11 David Handschuh/New York Daily News Archive/Getty Images; pp.4–5 Digital Vision/Getty Images; pp.6 (top), 9, 19 (right), 24 (right) The Granger Collection, NYC/The Granger Collection; pp.12 (top), 14–15, 27, 29 (bottom) iStock; p.20 LOC, LC-USZ62-105246; p.12 (bottom) LOC, LC-USZC2-1755; p.10 LOC, LC-USZC4-4940 The Library of Congress; p.25 Everett Collection/Newscom; pp.2–3 ZumaPress/Newscom; p.7 (left) North Wind Picture Archives; all other images from Shutterstock.

Library of Congress Cataloging-in-Publication Data

Dustman, Jeanne.
  American culture / Jeanne Dustman, M.A.Ed.
    pages cm
  Includes index.
  ISBN 978-1-4333-7360-2 (pbk.)
  ISBN 978-1-4807-5146-0 (ebook)
  1. United States—Civilization--Juvenile literature.
  2. United States—Social life and customs—
Juvenile literature. I. Title.
  E169.1.D89 2014
  973--dc23

                                        2014010234

Teacher Created Materials

5301 Oceanus Drive
Huntington Beach, CA 92649-1030
http://www.tcmpub.com
ISBN 978-1-4333-7360-2

Table of Contents

American Mosaic

When groups of people live together, they create their own ways of doing things. They may share similar **customs**. They may have similar **beliefs**. People create a way of life that is common to those in their group. This is called **culture**. Clothing, food, and arts are all part of culture. Some cultures may listen to a certain type of music. Others may make a special kind of art. Different cultures may celebrate different holidays. Each culture is unique.

Mosaic Art

A mosaic is a kind of art. It is made by pressing small pieces of colored stone or glass into a soft material. When the soft material dries, you have a beautiful picture or pattern.

America has a culture all its own. It is a large country with a rich history. It is made up of many different kinds of people. America's culture is like a mosaic (moh-ZEY-ik). It uses many small pieces to make one big, beautiful picture. That is to say, many cultures mix together to create the mosaic of an American way of life.

American Indian Culture

The first people to create rich cultures in America were the American Indians. Each **tribe**, or group of American Indians, had its own unique culture. But all tribes had great respect for the land. They believed the land supplied them with everything they needed to survive.

Each tribe had a different way of life. The tribes in the Northeast planted corn. It was their main crop. The Plains Indians lived in earth lodges or tepees. The tribes from the Southeast cherished family ties. Each family held a set of beliefs that was passed down to the next **generation** (jen-uh-REY-shuhn).

A Painful Time

American Indians were not treated well by the American government. In the 1800s, tribes were forced to leave their land. This led to bloody battles. Many American Indians also died from sickness during their forced moves.

American Indians created art, too. The Pueblo (PWEB-loh) tribes made beautiful pottery. The tribes of the Northwest were famous for their totem poles that tell their family histories.

American Indian cultures have changed over time. But the tribes have worked hard to save many of their **traditions** (truh-DISH-uhnz). They are a vital piece in the mosaic of American culture.

Northwestern tribes made totem poles to tell stories.

This Pueblo tribe grinds corn.

American Dream

The American dream is an important part of American culture. It is the idea that anyone who works hard can be successful and happy. It does not matter where you come from. You might not have any money. You may be the first person in your family to go to college. Or you may have come to America from another country. You can still achieve the American dream.

The dream promises that although today may be hard, tomorrow can always be better. It promises freedom, hope, and a new way of life.

This is an Italian immigrant family in 1905.

Ellis Island

Long ago, immigrants entered America through Ellis Island. It is near the Statue of Liberty in New York. It was an immigration station. Today it is a museum where you can learn about immigration.

This idea is one reason many **immigrants** (IM-i-gruhntz) came to America. Years ago, a large number of immigrants traveled to America. They came from all over the world. They left their homes and belongings. They left their friends and families. They hoped to make better lives for themselves. They believed in the American dream.

The immigrants who came to America had cultures of their own. They brought their customs and beliefs. They ate different kinds of food. They danced to different types of music. They celebrated their own holidays.

Immigrants shared their cultures with Americans. Over time, these cultures became part of American culture. Have you ever eaten a slice of pizza? Pizza came from Italy. Have you ever danced to mariachi (mahr-ee-AH-chee) music? It came from Mexico. Have you been to a Chinese New Year parade? There is one in the city of San Francisco every year.

Immigrants continue to come to America. They want to succeed. They want to make better lives for themselves. They believe in the American dream. Immigrants help make our country stronger. They bring their talents and skills. They bring new ideas. In so many ways, immigrants make America what it is today. They are one more important piece in the mosaic that is American culture.

Famous Immigrants

There are many famous immigrants. One of the most famous is Albert Einstein (AHYN-stahyn). He came to America from Germany. He brought with him his brilliant ideas about space and time.

Cinco de Mayo is a Mexican celebration.

American Society

American culture is a mosaic. But there are some parts of American society that started in America.

Fashion

Americans dress in all different styles. But there is some clothing that is truly American.

Cowboy hats and boots are **icons** of American fashion. Cowboys first wore them when they rode their horses. The hats kept the sun off the cowboys' faces and necks. The boots protected their feet from the hard ground.

Sturdy Strauss

Levi Strauss came to America from Europe in 1843. He knew gold miners needed sturdy pants that would not tear. So, Strauss designed jeans for them. Today, his jeans are known as Levi's jeans and you can still buy them in stores!

This painting shows gold miners wearing jeans in 1871.

When people in other countries think of American clothing, many think of denim (DEN-uhm) jeans. Denim is a strong cotton cloth. Denim jeans were first made popular in America in the 1800s. They were made to be work pants. Gold miners were the first to wear them. Over time, jeans became popular with teenagers and young adults. By the 1980s, designers were making more stylish jeans. Today, jeans are not only popular in America; people around the world wear them. Each season, there are new styles of jeans to wear.

These men wear different kinds of jeans.

Food

Many people think of hamburgers and hot dogs as American foods. But really they began in Germany. Americans did not invent apple pie, either. But, it has been a favorite dessert among many Americans for a long time. Americans have put their own spin on a variety of foods. However, there are some foods that are uniquely American.

Clam chowder is a favorite American food. It began on the east coast. It is easy to find clams there. Plus, the soup tastes good on the cold days that are common in that part of the country.

Chocolate Chip Cookies

The first chocolate chip cookie was made by an American woman in the 1930s. She sold her recipe to Nestlé (NES-lee). This company made chocolate bars. Nestlé paid her with a lifetime supply of chocolate!

Many Southern states are known for their famous barbeque (BAHR-bi-kyoo). Barbeque is meat that is cooked over an open fire. A sauce is used to add extra flavor. There are many kinds of barbeque sauce. Texan barbeque sauce is tangy and spicy. Memphis-style sauce is sweet. This is because it uses molasses. Molasses is a thick, brown liquid that is made from raw sugar.

What is your favorite food? Is it from America?

Music

Most cultures have their own styles of music. They help us express ourselves. They tell our stories. Music can make us feel everything from happy to sad. It can also make you excited or calm. Some styles of music started in America. Others came from immigrants who shared their cultures.

blues artist, B. B. King

ELVIS
PRESLEY

MORE THAN
100 PICTURES
•
PRESLEY'S
COMPLETE
LIFE STORY
•
FERVID
FANS
•
RECORD
RECORDINGS
•
EXCLUSIVE
ELVIS' FIRST
SCREEN TEST

All Shook Up!

Elvis Presley is one of the most famous American music performers of all time. He was born in Mississippi on January 9, 1935. His mother bought him his first guitar when he was 11 years old. Later, he would make 150 albums.

Today, there are more genres (ZHAHN-ruhz), or types, of music than ever before. African Americans created many of these American genres of music. Blues helped African Americans share their culture. So did gospel and jazz. Then, these different genres of music inspired rock and roll. Rock and roll is one of the most popular types of music to come out of America. Other popular music forms include rap and hip-hop. African Americans created these music genres, as well. Country music began in America, too.

Folklore

Every culture has **folklore**. Folklore is told from person to person and is passed down over time. American folklore is about America and its people. It includes songs, stories, myths, rhymes, sayings, and traditions. Many stories are about the people who first settled America. These stories may or may not be true. But they are always entertaining.

Paul Bunyan

Paul Bunyan (BUHN-yuhn) is a famous American folklore hero. He was a huge, strong man who could move giant logs with ease. His enormous blue ox named Babe was always with him. Together they created the Grand Canyon and built the Rocky Mountains.

Johnny Appleseed is famous in American folklore. He was said to have traveled the country planting apple seeds. This story is based on a real man named John Chapman. Chapman did plant apple seeds. But not as many as Johnny Appleseed did.

This is a drawing of what Johnny Appleseed may have looked like.

This statue of Johnny Appleseed is an ad for a restaurant.

19

Sports

Americans love sports. We like playing them. We like watching them. Two of the biggest sports in America are football and baseball.

Football is the most popular sport in our country. It started in America in the 1860s. Today, many kids play football. They play it in high school and college, too. People also like to watch professional, or pro, football. Pro players get paid money to play a sport.

Baseball is the oldest team sport in America. Baseball as we know it today started in America in the early 1800s. For many years, only white men were allowed to play in the major leagues. But in 1947, Jackie Robinson changed that. He was the first African American player in Major League Baseball. Today, athletes are welcomed into Major League Baseball regardless of skin color.

Batter Up!

Babe Ruth is one of the most famous American baseball players of all time. He was a great hitter. He was the first player to hit 60 home runs in one season.

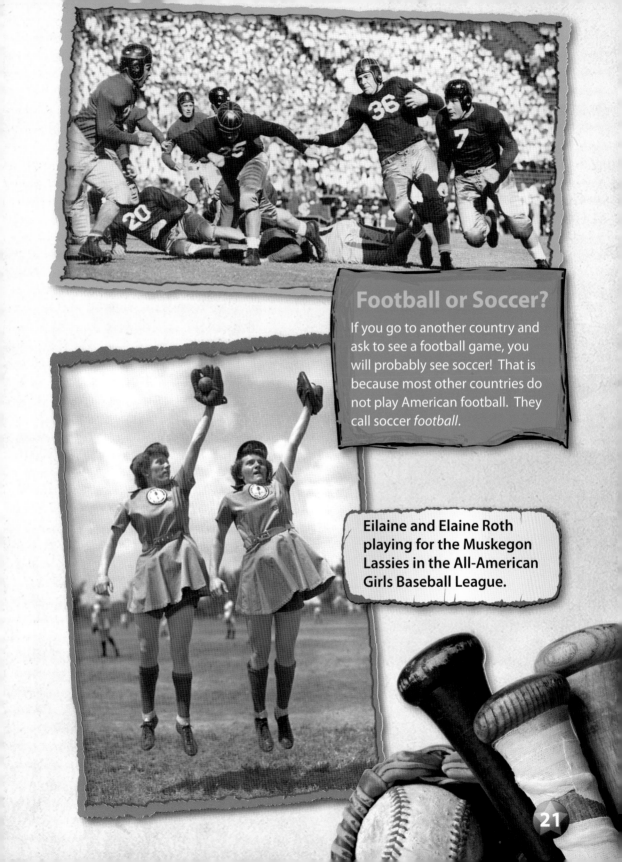

Football or Soccer?

If you go to another country and ask to see a football game, you will probably see soccer! That is because most other countries do not play American football. They call soccer *football*.

Eilaine and Elaine Roth playing for the Muskegon Lassies in the All-American Girls Baseball League.

Celebrations

American culture has many holidays. These are special days. They each honor something that Americans think is important.

The Fourth of July is America's birthday! It is also called **Independence** (in-di-PEN-duhns) Day. Every year, we honor the day America became a country. This happened in 1776. Today, we enjoy food with family and friends. We watch fireworks. And we sing **patriotic** songs.

These people celebrate the Fourth of July.

This family enjoys eating Thanksgiving dinner together.

These kids honor veterans at a parade.

Another big holiday is Thanksgiving Day. This happens in November. It started as a way to celebrate the harvest. This is the time when food is gathered from the fields. Today, many people see it as a time to say what they are thankful for. It is also a day to spend time with family. Many people eat turkey for dinner. And they eat pumpkin pie for dessert.

Veterans (VET-er-uhns) Day happens every November 11. On this day, we thank the men and women in the military who help keep our country safe. We have parades. We listen to speeches.

All these holidays help us remember what we think is important.

Land of the Free, Home of the Brave

An important part of American culture is our country's history. The story of America is the story of us. America is a free country. But it was not always free. America used to be 13 **colonies**. The king of Great Britain ruled the colonies. The colonies had to fight a long war against Great Britain. This is called the *American Revolution*. The colonies fought hard for their freedom. And they won! But not all people were free.

Americans fight for their freedom in the Battle of Bunker Hill.

These slaves are forced to cut down sugar cane on a plantation.

Slavery is an awful part of America's story. Slaves were people who were forced to work without pay. They had no freedom. Another person owned them. Slaves were treated very poorly. It took another long war to end slavery in America. This war is called the Civil War.

After the Civil War, all Americans were free. But not everyone was treated equally. Women, African Americans, and other groups had to fight for their **civil rights**. They have fought bravely and have never given up!

Land of Leaders

America is a land of leaders. George Washington led America to freedom during the American Revolution. Abraham Lincoln led America during the Civil War and helped end slavery. Elizabeth Cady Stanton and Susan B. Anthony led women and helped them get the right to vote. Dr. Martin Luther King Jr. led African Americans during the civil rights movement.

Dr. Martin Luther King Jr. gives a speech.

American **values** come from our country's history. Americans value freedom. We honor bravery. We respect hard work. We believe in freedom of speech. We think that every person has the power and right to make his or her own decisions. While denim jeans and baseball games may be symbols of America, these core values are what truly define American culture.

These men show their pride by painting the American flag.

This soldier's family is proud of his bravery.

America is made up of many different types of people. This is one of the great things about our country. It is a nation built on ideas brought here from around the world. It makes American culture unique. We are all different. But we are all Americans. Each one of us is a piece in the mosaic of American culture. We must treat everyone equally. We must treat everyone with respect. This is the American way of life!

Make It!

What is one of your favorite parts of American culture? Think of an image that represents that part. Then make a mosaic. Tear or cut different colored sheets of paper into tiny pieces. Use those pieces to create one image that represents your favorite part of American culture.

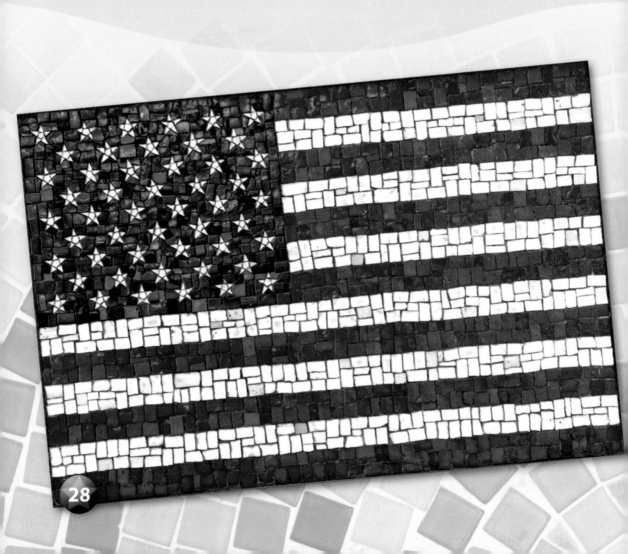

These students make
paper mosaics.

Glossary

beliefs—feelings that something is true or right

civil rights—rights that every person should have

colonies—areas ruled by another country

culture—the characteristics of everyday life shared by a group of people in a particular place or time

customs—ways of behaving that are usual among people in a particular place

folklore—stories and sayings handed down from generation to generation

generation—a group of people born and living during the same time

icons—a widely known symbol

immigrants—people who move to another country to live there

independence—freedom from outside control or support

patriotic—having and showing love and support for your country

traditions—ways of thinking or doing things that have been done by a particular group for a long time

tribe—a group of people who have the same language, customs, and beliefs

values—strongly held beliefs about what is important

Index

Your Turn!

Life in America

What does American culture mean to you? What parts of American culture play a role in your daily life? Write a short paragraph about American culture in your life. Use the text in this book to support your ideas.

American Culture

Jeanne Dustman